China Stories

A PRAYER GUIDE

Copyright © 2012, OMF International
Published by OMF International
10 West Dry Creek Circle, Littleton CO 80120
ISBN-13: 978-1-929122-43-1
ISBN-10: 1-92912243-8
This printing 2012

OMF BOOKS

Visit *www.OMFBooks.com* for more information.

Chinese Provinces

Xinjiang*

(Ir

Qinghai

G

Xizang*
(Tibet)

Sich

Yunnan

Heilongjiang

Jilin

Liaoning

Hebei
Beijing

⬅l*
olia)

Tianjin

Shanxi

Shandong

Jiangsu

anxi

Henan

Anhui

Shanghai

Hubei

Zhejiang

Hunan

Jiangxi

Fujian

ou

Guangdong

uangxi*

Hong Kong

Hainan

Home to 1.3 billion people and one of the world's fastest growing economies, China is one of the most influential countries in the world. It is also home to one of the fastest growing church movements in the world. God is at work in powerful ways in this ancient land. Yet, the needs are still great. More than 1 billion Chinese still do not know Christ. The dynamic Chinese church is experiencing growing pains. Social change is producing massive upheaval in Chinese society. In the following pages are stories of hope and need. As you read, lift up China in prayer and join God's work in this Asian giant.

* Autonomous Region

Living in a Material World

Coming from a poor farmer's family in Henan Province, Wei Feng dreamed of attaining "the good life." For him, that meant a good education, followed by a high-paying job, a pretty wife and a comfortable lifestyle—in short, nothing like his hard upbringing in China's heartland.

Against all odds, Wei Feng succeeded in attaining all of that. As a child, he studied hard and scored well on the college entrance exam, high enough to attend a prestigious university. After graduation, he went to Hong Kong for his MBA, followed by securing a lucrative job with an American company operating in China. A few years ago, he married his long-term, live-in girlfriend, Sun Ling. They live in a spacious high rise apartment in Shanghai.

Wei Feng had it all. He advanced to the executive level of his job. He made more money than he ever dreamed. He and Sun Ling vacationed every spring in Hainan Island, China's "Hawaii." He drove a shiny BMW and was the envy of his friends back home.

But he still had a nagging sense of emptiness. Wei Feng had everything, but was unfulfilled. His pursuit of material excess temporarily satisfied his physical needs but left a constant gnawing in his soul.

Materialism is quickly supplanting atheism, Communism and Confucianism as the dominant worldview in China. China's unprecedented economic growth has had many positive results (for example, almost universally raising the standard of living in the country), but this has come at a great cost as well.

The spiritual vacuum created by decades of atheism once made for fertile ground for the gospel. Now, however, many are turning to the enticements of materialism instead. As seen by its effect on the West, materialism is powerful in its ability to keep people in spiritual darkness. It leads to a self-perpetuating cycle of pursuing wealth and accumulating more.

Whatever it takes—cheating, bribing or sacrificing family life—it doesn't matter as long as it helps one get ahead. But the fallout can be harsh: mass corruption driven by greed, broken marriages, and dissension between poor and rich.

Sadly, materialism is influencing some in the church as well, whether through the preaching of an unbiblical health-and-wealth gospel or through distracting believers from the eternal treasure of Christ with the temporal treasures of this world.

Thankfully for Wei Feng, God used his restlessness to draw him to Christ. Looking for answers that atheism and materialism couldn't provide, Wei Feng began reading the Bible at the urging of a Christian neighbor. He previously thought Christianity was an outdated foreign religion, but now saw how precious the Good News really was. God has transformed his life. He now lives not for himself, but Christ and his purposes. May many others follow his example in turning from the idols of materialism to the living God.

唯物主义

Pray for the Affluent

"Do not store up for yourselves treasures on earth, where moth and rust destroy, and where thieves break in and steal. But store up for yourselves treasures in heaven, … For where your treasure is, there your heart will be also."
Matthew 6:19-21

» Intercede for the Chinese people, asking that they would not be blinded by the allures of material excess.

» Pray that biblical values of generosity and serving others would supplant self-seeking materialism.

» Ask for God's protection over the Chinese church, that the prosperity "gospel" would not take root. The Chinese church has long been a model of embracing suffering and the cross for the advance of the gospel. May it continue to be so.

"Because I am a Christian"

Mary dreamed of being a nurse. She hoped by doing so she could help people in her small, poor town in Southwest China. Although nursing school costs were too high for her family to afford, some Christian friends sponsored her so she could go to school and realize her dream.

As Mary spent time with these friends, she observed how they applied their Christian faith in the workplace. They didn't just talk about Jesus and the Bible. They lived out his teachings, including caring for others. Eventually, Mary and her two sisters came to faith in Jesus.

Later, when Mary was a nurse intern, she noticed an old man in the hospital who was very lonely and dirty. He had five children who paid his hospital bills, but never came to visit him. In China, it is the duty of family members—not the nurses—to take care of patients' personal needs. Mary, however, took compassion on this old man and cared for him even though it was not her duty.

One day, she asked him what he would like to eat. His simple request was noodles. Mary bought the noodles and started to feed him strand by strand. Her simple kindness moved him very deeply. He cried out: "Why are you do-ing this? Even my own children do not take care of me!" Mary's simple reply was, "I do this because I am a Christian." She then led the old man to Christ. A few days later, he passed away.

Mary modeled holistic ministry. Out of her love for Christ, she loved others and was willing to go the extra mile in her service. Holistic ministry results when Christians do their work in such a way that it provokes the kind of questions to which the gospel is the only answer.

Christian doctors, nurses and other professionals have the opportunity to use their skills and training to make an eternal impact for the gospel in hard-to-reach places. As patients experience a high standard of care and see healing in their bodies, they are more receptive to the gospel that can heal their soul.

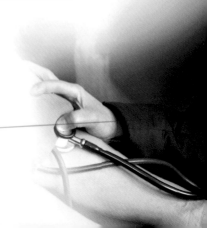

Although Christians in China face many restrictions to openly sharing the gospel in their workplace, no law can stop them from being like Christ in their professional service. How great it will be to see millions of Chinese Christians work and serve like Mary so that others will ask, "Why are you doing this?", and hear, "We do this because we are Christians. We do this because we come in the spirit of Christ."

事奉

Pray for the Servants

Let your conversation be always full of grace, seasoned with salt, so that you may know how to answer everyone.
Colossians 4:6

» Pray that holistic ministry efforts related to medical work and community development will bless communities and bear eternal fruit.

» Ask God to raise up more Chinese Christians like Mary to witness in their workplace and communities.

» Pray for foreign and Chinese Christians to be Christ-like models to their co-workers and those they serve. May they demonstrate the truth that "the greatest among you will be your servant" (Matthew 23:11).

» Pray for nonbelievers to ask questions about selfless, Christ-driven service they witness or experience.

Passing on the Faith

Jin Hua's father is a key leader among Chinese house churches. Now over 80 years old, he was imprisoned in the 1950s and again during the Cultural Revolution because of his faith in Christ. When he was released from prison in the late seventies, it was a time of revival among rural house churches in China. God used him to minister to many young leaders of the churches.

Jin Hua is now in his early forties. Growing up in a family whose father was considered an outcast by the government, he did not have an easy childhood. But he shares the fervent faith of his father, from whom he learned to trust God despite difficult circumstances.

After completing his theological education overseas, Jin Hua returned to China with the vision of church planting in the mostly unreached northwest part of China. The first church he planted has grown to four churches today.

God then led Jin Hua to start a theological seminary in partnership with some foreign workers in 2001. The seminary, which was established to train mission-minded pastors and church leaders, recently celebrated its tenth anniversary. In addition to a Master's degree in Christian Studies, the seminary also offers leadership classes for bi-vocational Christian leaders. The seminary has produced four classes of graduates who have spread throughout China—some with large, rural house-church networks, others with urban churches.

The need for theological training in China is great. Among the official, government-recognized Three-Self Patriotic Movement (TSPM) churches, there are only 23 theological schools in the whole country, meaning there is just one ordained pastor for every 10,000 believers in the Three-Self churches. That doesn't include the house churches that the majority of Chinese believers attend.

To compensate for the dearth in theological training, many house-church networks have set up their own unofficial seminaries. In addition, more and more Chinese Christians are seeking theological training overseas, outside of China. The zeal of Chinese believers is strong, but zeal without adequate knowledge of Scripture has occasionally led to the proliferation of cults, such as Eastern Lightning. Furthermore, a lack of grounding in the Bible has also contributed to a lack of deep, sustained commitment among new believers, leading to nominal belief in some cases.

Seminaries like Jin Hua's, however, give hope that more Chinese believers will be well-versed in the truths of the Bible to address doctrinal error and to equip believers to more adequately and confidently teach and share their faith with others.

神学

Pray for the Seminaries

And the things you have heard me say in the presence of many witnesses entrust to reliable men who will also be qualified to teach others.
2 Timothy 2:2

» Praise God for the faith and sacrifice of Chinese believers like Jin Hua and his father. May their lives be models to a new generation of the Chinese church.

» Pray against the enemy who seeks to distort truth. Ask God to protect seekers and new Christians from the influence of cults and nominal belief.

» Ask for God's help and leading in the establishment of more seminaries and Bible schools throughout China, leading to more theologically sound and equipped pastors and leaders for the church in China.

The Great Migration

Zhou Li and her family live in temporary housing with other migrant workers from rural China. They live simply and save as much money as possible. After first arriving in the city, Zhou Li bounced around from various jobs at shops and markets, until she finally landed steady work as a nanny and housekeeper. The 30-year-old wife and mother works hard and cheerfully at her job. Her husband works long hours as a construction worker, joining the millions of other migrant workers who build China's cities.

Though originally from the countryside of Anhui Province in Central China, Zhou Li has adjusted to big city life. Even so, she and her husband hope one day to return to her home village and buy a nice house with the money they have earned in the city. Their daughter, Li Mei, goes to a migrant school in Beijing. Compared to Beijing's "normal" schools, conditions and standards are lower, but Zhou Li seems pleased with the progress her daughter is making.

She's not pleased, however, with the prospect of sending her back to Anhui for middle and high school. As the child of a migrant worker, Li Mei is not legally registered in Beijing. She cannot attend official Beijing schools because her residency card (an identification card that dictates one's hometown) states that she is from Anhui. Migrant schools try to meet the need for education, but they are sometimes shut down without notice by authorities.

Adjusting to urban life, in sometimes dilapidated living conditions, is common fare for China's migrant population—over 250 million people by the latest official estimates.[1] In recent decades, China has gone through a massive human migration. Whereas before the vast majority of the Middle Kingdom's population lived in rural areas, the number of city dwellers is perpetually climbing. In 2011, urbanites came to represent the majority of the Chinese population.[2]

China's economic development has been the catalyst for the change. As China opened up and more factories were built in places like the Pearl River Delta in southern China, rural workers flooded the cities looking for better pay and a better life.

The result has meant an upheaval in Chinese society. Once populous villages are now home only to the elderly and

---

1 *www.msnbc.msn.com*, 01.17.12.
2 Ibid.

small children. In the cities, migrants work for low wages with few benefits such as insurance or pensions. The wealth divide between most migrants and China's emerging middle and upper classes has created social problems. Some blame migrants for an increase in crime and disease.

For Zhou Li, the greatest difficulty has been leaving her hometown and being separated from her extended family. In a few years when her daughter is old enough to go back and attend middle school in their home province, the loss will be more acute. Zhou Li hopes the sacrifice is worth it.

Some churches and ministries are making efforts to reach out to migrants, providing practical help while also introducing them to Jesus, but the migrant population is so big that much work remains.

移民

Pray for the Migrants

When he saw the crowds, he had compassion on them, because they were harassed and helpless, like sheep without a shepherd.
Matthew 9:36

» Pray for the government to have wisdom and deal fairly with the millions of migrants in China's big cities.

» Pray for urban churches to reach out and welcome migrants in their communities, showing them the love of Christ.

» Intercede for the preservation and unity of Chinese families affected by urban migration.

» Ask God for spiritual openness and receptiveness by migrant workers to the gospel of Christ.

A Mix of Beliefs

Li Jiao was raised most of her childhood by her grandparents in southern China. She is outgoing, independent and strong willed. About 10 years ago, she moved to Beijing for college. While there, she made friends with several foreigners, including some Christians. Li Jiao quickly latched on to the foreigners' new "philosophy," as she called it. She immersed herself in the Bible, soaking in its wisdom and history.

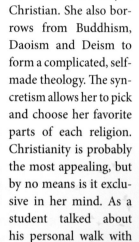

Li Jiao is now a successful Chinese teacher. Students love her. She keeps class lively and engaging. When asked about her teaching philosophy, Li Jiao cites Paul's letter to the Corinthians: "To the weak I became weak, to win the weak. I have become all things to all people so that by all possible means I might save some" (1 Corinthians 9:22). She tries to discern her students' learning styles and aptitudes and adjust class accordingly.

When discussing leadership theories one day in class, Li Jiao rebuked a Christian student who had been studying a variety of books and articles related to the topic. "You don't need to read leadership books," she said. "You just need to read the Bible because Jesus is the greatest leader in history."

When asked about her faith, Li Jiao replies that she is a Christian. Given her knowledge of scripture, that is not surprising.

Probing further, however, reveals some problems. Li Jiao isn't only a Christian. She also borrows from Buddhism, Daoism and Deism to form a complicated, self-made theology. The syncretism allows her to pick and choose her favorite parts of each religion. Christianity is probably the most appealing, but by no means is it exclusive in her mind. As a student talked about his personal walk with Christ one day, Li Jiao interjected.

"You think a personal relationship with God is important?" she asked quizzically.

The student answered in the affirmative, explaining the significance of the incarnation of Christ and a litany of Bible verses that speak of the need for deep, loving and personal interaction with the maker of the universe.

Li Jiao disagreed. "Only belief is enough," she asserted. In the future, she quickly shut down any conversation that might lead to someone challenging the logic of her beliefs. She very rarely attends church.

Many stories about the growth of Christianity in China refer to the commitment and fervor of Chinese believers. They know their Bibles and are orthodox and evangelical in their beliefs. Thankfully, this is often true. But not always. There are many nominal, quasi-Christians who assert Christian values and wisdom without following or endorsing the way of Jesus wholeheartedly.

This speaks to the need for more biblical training and life-on-life discipleship. As China has opened up to the outside world, a flood of idolatrous religions have entered alongside Christianity in the battle for people's hearts. Rather than basing faith on biblical truths, many, like Li Jiao, mix-and-match tenets from disparate worldviews. Foundationally, it's a self-centered approach that wants what religion can do for them without considering the demands of God.

Pray for Devotion

Not everyone who says to me, 'Lord, Lord,' will enter the kingdom of heaven, but only he who does the will of my Father who is in heaven.
Matthew 7:21

» Pray for more biblical training and discipleship of new believers to ground them so that they will not be easily swayed from the true gospel.

» Ask for Holy Spirit-led conviction and repentance by nominal believers to fully embrace the gospel truths.

» Pray against self-centered syncretism and half-hearted belief that produces no transformation.

» Pray that many would embrace Christ fully and not dismiss Christianity as just a "western religion to be studied."

Introducing the Good Shepherd

"The view from the mountain is beautiful, but the climb is difficult," Xu Wei thought to himself as he labored up the mountainside to his home village. The combined effects of old age and a childhood case of polio that left him lame in one of his legs made the journey especially arduous.

Xu Wei, who belongs to one of China's minority people groups, has lived all his life in a remote mountain village in western China. He is poor and illiterate, just like all the other adults in the village. Some of the children—who may attend school up to third grade in a nearby village—can read a little.

One day a group of Chinese and foreign visitors came to the village. "How did they find us up here?" Xu Wei wondered. The village was one of the last remaining settlements on the mountain as the government was trying to get villagers to move to the city in the valley below. Xu Wei wouldn't mind relocating, actually, but could not afford to do so.

The team of Chinese and foreigners offered to help Xu Wei's village. With one of the greatest needs being literacy, the Chinese—at the request of the village's leader—started a weekly class teaching the villagers how to read Mandarin. Every weekend, the team traversed up the mountain, taught classes and spent the night in the village.

The team also started a sheep loan project for the village. As the people in the village raised the sheep, they could keep any lambs born and sell them for income. Xu Wei and the other villagers agreed this was a good plan and began caring for the sheep. Thankfully, there was plenty of grazing land for the sheep to eat.

The bond between the villagers and team quickly grew. The village appreciated the team's genuine concern for them. The quality of life in the village improved.

Over time, the team shared why they wanted to help the people of the village. They were compelled to do good to others because of God's love for them—and all people—they said. When they stayed in the villagers' homes, they shared stories from their holy book, the Bible, about a Savior named Jesus. They sometimes prayed to Jesus for Xu Wei and other sick or ailing members of the village. Amazingly, Xu Wei's leg began feeling better.

Xu Wei, who became the group's main contact in the village, found the message intriguing. The visitors eventually gave Xu Wei a copy of the *Jesus* film, which he watched intently … and repeatedly. In fact, he watched the film so much that he memorized large portions of it. He even wondered if the movie's message was true—that Jesus really was God and the Savior of the world.

发 展

Pray for Developments

"The King will reply, 'I tell you the truth, whatever you did for one of the least of these brothers of mine, you did for me.'"
Matthew 25:40

» Ask for God to grant those involved in community development in China compassion and creativity as to how to provide long-term viable aid.

» Pray for open doors to share the gospel in impoverished and overlooked communities. May people's hearts be soft toward the life-giving message of God's grace.

» Pray for development and relief efforts on the part of Christian workers to be effective in alleviating poverty and improving the quality of life for those they serve.

Climbing Mandarin Mountain

It is 7:50 a.m. Another day of Chinese class awaits. Tom gathers his books and heads out the door. Downstairs, he waves at the door lady.

"*Zao* (good morning)," she says with a smile.

In case he had forgotten, this is the day's first reminder that he is in China. On the short walk to the language school, he passes a group of old people using fake swords to do their morning *tai-qi* exercises. He is definitely in China.

Tom arrives at the school at 8:00 a.m. sharp, usually at the same time as his teacher, whose English name is Mary. Neither one of them is "a morning person" but within a few minutes Mary is her friendly, ever-corrective-of-his-Chinese self. Today, they were starting a new lesson, which meant new vocabulary. In the cycle of the lessons, this is Tom's favorite day.

Tom opens his book and begins repeating each word Mary says.

"*Pingshi,*" she begins.

Oh no, two second tones in a row! This is one of Tom's weaknesses. He concentrates … "*Pingshi.*"

"*Piiinng,*" Mary says, exaggerating it to let him know he didn't get his tone high enough.

"Okay, … *Piiinngshiii,*" Tom replies, feeling silly.

"*Feichang hao* (very good)," she says. Tom is not sure he believes her.

"Translate for me," she says. "There are a lot of Australians at that university."

"When will I ever say that?" Tom thinks to himself, before beginning the translation process. There are … probably have to use "*you*" (pronounced "yo") and maybe "*zai.*" Oh yes, "*zai.*" Another weakness. It seemingly has about 30 different meanings in Chinese. Tom decides he's going to try to get by without it this time.

"*Neige daxue you hen duo Aodaliyaren,*" he says sheepishly.

"*Dui* (correct)" she says.

YESSS!!! They say to celebrate your "language victories" as a means of encouragement and Tom needs all the encouragement he can get. Today is going to be a good "Chinese day" (meaning he will be able to speak and comprehend better than usual). He can feel it.

"Next sentence," says Mary, interrupting his positive thoughts. "I haven't played basketball for two months."

"Okay, I got this," Tom thinks to himself. "*Wo mei da lanqiu liang ge yue,*" he says, confidently this time.

The look on Mary's face says it all. "Should you put '*liang ge yue*' before or after '*mei*'?" she asks. Tom now knows he is wrong, but decides to protest anyway.

"But 'time spent' phrases go after the verb, don't they?" he inquires.

"Not if it's negative time spent," says Mary.

"Right ... should've known that," Tom chides himself. "That was one of last week's lessons."

After two hours, class is over. Tom is excited about the new words he now knows, but once again he feels humbled by his lack of mastery of this language. It's like being a child again.

Once when discussing a colleague's name in class, Tom had told Mary the name was "*Xiao* (3rd tone) *Ji* (1st tone)." She nearly jumped out of her chair.

"Don't say that! You're calling her a small chicken!" Whoops. These moments happen all the time.

It's time to return home and immerse himself in learning the new vocabulary. First, he tells Mary goodbye.

"*Zaijian* (goodbye)," he says. "Wait a minute ... I can use "*zai*" correctly. There is hope!"

外国人

Pray for the Foreigner

That is why it was called Babel—because there the Lord confused the language of the whole world. From there the Lord scattered them over the face of the whole earth.
Genesis 11:9

» Lift up foreign Christian workers learning Chinese. May they persevere in learning a complex language and have the clarity of mind to grasp and use Chinese to relate to the Chinese people in their native tongue.

» Pray for the effective use of Chinese for the advance of the gospel in China.

» Ask God to give Chinese teachers insight, patience and creativity as they teach foreign students.

» Pray for appropriate, spirit-led contextualization as Chinese and foreign Christians spread the gospel in China.

Will Fear Always Hold Her Back?

Xiao Ma hails from a beautiful town situated on the Silk Road where Islam first entered China. On the third day after she was born, her parents invited an *ahong* (imam) to their home for a "Naming Ceremony" during which he gave Xiao Ma her Muslim name, *Miriam* (Mary).

Growing up under intense Islamic influence, Xiao Ma heard the call to prayer from the mosque five times a day. Her father's white hat and mother's black veil were a constant reminder of her Muslim heritage. As a child, she recited the Qur'an with neighborhood friends in one of the many conspicuous mosques dominating the landscape in her home town. "No matter how difficult and painstaking it is to learn Arabic, it is the most beautiful language given by Allah!" she was told.

After graduating from high school, Xiao Ma left home for the first time and attended college in the provincial capital. Before she left, her father sternly warned her, "Never forget that you are a Muslim!" While attending foreign language class, she was fascinated with learning about a new culture. She was thrilled to receive her first Christmas stocking filled with chocolates and some months later, a colorful, decorated Easter egg.

Later, Xiao Ma saw the *Jesus* Film. After watching, her surprisingly heated question was, "Why are you foreigners trying to get us to change our religion?"

Slowly, after 18 months, Xiao Ma let her guard down. She borrowed a Bible from the school library and studied it one-on-one with a Christian for a full year. Then, sadly, Xiao Ma unexpectedly stopped attending the weekly meetings. After many months, she finally shared the struggle in her heart. "I was born to be a Muslim and believe in Islam. That cannot be changed. In the past years, I was at peace, but since you started sharing many things about Jesus with me, I have become confused and perplexed. I feel under pressure. I do not want to offend Allah. Therefore, I will not come and listen to stories about Jesus or sing those songs anymore."

China is home to 20 million Muslims and more than 100 million minorities overall. These minority groups represent a diverse array of cultures and religions. Some, like the Hui and Uyghur, embrace Islam. Others, like Tibetans and the Shan, follow Buddhism, while others, particularly in southwestern China, adhere to animistic and folk traditions. A few—the Lisu, for example—have been transformed by the gospel of Jesus Christ. Many who have heard the gospel in these groups, however, are like Xiao Ma—fearful and bound by tradition.

少数民族
Pray for Minorities

Jesus answered, "I am the way and the truth and the life. No one comes to the Father except through me."
John 14:6

» Pray for Xiao Ma and others like her among China's minority peoples to be freed by Jesus Christ from fear and idolatrous traditions.

» Ask God for guidance, boldness and wisdom for Chinese and foreign Christians seeking to share the gospel and plant churches in China's minority groups.

» Intercede for minority Christians to have courage and perseverance in the midst of possible persecution from family and friends for their faith in Christ.

Students in Despair

The phone kept ringing with no answer. After a long time, Tim hung up, hoping his friend, Peng, was okay.

Tim had met with Peng just a few days earlier. They were language partners, meaning they met once a week so Peng could practice English and Tim could practice Chinese. They had been meeting for more than a year. Peng's English was excellent.

Conversations sometimes included talking about the Bible. Though not yet a believer, Peng was quite insightful. When discussing the story of Job, Peng noted that he thought the book's point was "Will you trust God even in the hard times?" Still, though he showed interest in spiritual matters, he was noncommittal.

Now in his senior year of college, Peng hoped to go to graduate school. He preferred to go abroad, but he did not have enough money. Instead, Peng decided to attend a Chinese university for his graduate studies. When Tim saw Peng last, however, he had just learned that he failed to make the necessary test score to proceed with his graduate plans. He was discouraged.

Several days later, Tim heard a report of a student at Peng's university jumping to his death. The profile of the student seemed to fit Peng: a senior male who had failed the test to enter graduate school.

Alarmed, Tim immediately called Peng's cell phone, to no avail. Now, he was *really* concerned. Though Peng was sad the last time they had met, he still seemed stable. But ... what if?

Suicide is the number one cause of death among Chinese young people (age 15-34), according to the Chinese Center for Disease Control and Prevention. An estimated 287,000 Chinese take their life each year; approximately 2 million make unsuccessful attempts to do so.[1]

It's common in the late spring, around final exam time, to hear stories of suicide among college students in China. For many, especially for those who come from rural areas, college is a way out—not only for them, but for their whole family. Getting accepted to a college, especially a more prestigious one, is a huge achievement. Such students are often the pride of their village. The pressure to succeed is immense. When they fail to do so, suicide often seems like the best option.

Tim couldn't help himself. Though it had only been a few minutes, he had to call again. Nervously, he highlighted Peng's name in his phone and pressed the send button. Again, lots of rings without an answer. Then, just as he was about to hang up, an obviously sleepy Peng angrily answered, "Wei?" (a common phone greeting in China).

1 Xinhua News Agency, 9.8.2011.

Tim could hardly contain his relief. "Peng!! You're alive!" is what he wanted to say, but instead apologized for waking Peng up and said something about trying to get together again the next week.

After hanging up, a wave of thankfulness came over Tim, followed by a renewed sense of urgency to share the gospel with Chinese college students who place all their hope in education, instead of the loving, unfailing God they were made to know.

学生

Pray for the Students

Why are you downcast, O my soul? Why so disturbed within me? Put your hope in God, for I will yet praise him, my Savior and my God.
Psalm 43:5

» Pray against Satan and his demons who seek to "kill, steal and destroy" (John 10:10) Chinese college students with hopeless and despairing thoughts and attitudes.

» Ask God to equip Christian students, professors and workers to be faithful witnesses and have listening hearts towards those in need of hope and encouragement.

» Ask God for wisdom on the part of counselors, parents, school administrators and governing authorities who are seeking to address this issue. May this saddening trend soon be reversed.

From China to the World

As a Chinese teacher, Xiao Yue has taught many foreign Christians "spiritual language," that is, vocabulary associated with sharing the gospel and discussing spiritual matters.

The exposure to foreign believers who have left their home country to share the gospel has made quite the impression on her. One day she may cross a culture herself.

"I don't know where yet, but I think God is calling me to be a missionary," she said.

Xiao Yue is one of a growing number of Chinese Christians thinking about their role in the Great Commission. Long seen as a missionary-receiving field, China may be on the cusp of becoming a missionary-sending country in the coming decades. A trickle of Chinese believers have already gone abroad to spread the gospel.

Much attention related to missions from China has gone to the Back to Jerusalem (BTJ) Movement. Dating to the 1920s, the BTJ Movement has been renewed in recent years, especially among some of China's rural house-church networks. Though some of the recent movement's claims and goals have come under controversy, several

house-church networks have set up mission-training centers for prospective Chinese missionaries. The plan is to start in China's western provinces, home to many of the country's minority groups and progress through Central Asia into the Middle East—eventually, back to Jerusalem, where the gospel began.

It should be noted, however, that the global missions movement within China is more complex than just Back to Jerusalem. Chinese church leaders hope to send missionaries in every direction—not just toward the Middle East. They also do not think they are alone in the completion of the Great Commission. Instead, they hope to partner with the global church.

Some believe the suffering and persecution endured by Chinese believers over the past few decades could be preparation for a future mission-sending movement. Chinese believers are acquainted with the costs of following Christ. Perhaps they will more readily embrace the hardships related to cross-cultural missions due to the difficulties faced in their own country.

For now, the missions movement from China is still in its infancy. Such a movement will be complicated by the fact that China is a Communist country. Parachurch mission organizations cannot exist openly, making the sending of missionaries perhaps more problematic.

One prominent house-church pastor thinks it may be his children's generation that will see a major missions movement from China. The growth of the church among Chinese urban intellectuals is a positive sign in the movement. Many of them have already been overseas, are well-acquainted with the global stage and can speak English. Perhaps the Chinese church could follow the pattern of the South Korean church which experienced explosive growth in the 1960s and 70s. Thirty years later, South Korea is the second-largest mission-sending country in the world.

宣教

Pray for Missions

Therefore go and make disciples of all nations, baptizing them in the name of the Father and of the Son and of the Holy Spirit, and teaching them to obey everything I have commanded you. And surely I am with you always, to the very end of the age.
Matthew 28:19-20

» Pray for more Chinese believers to have a desire to participate in the Great Commission.

» Ask for wisdom and direction as Chinese church leaders think about how to engage in global and cross-cultural mission.

» Lift up for Chinese believers like Xiao Yue who are considering cross-cultural mission. May they be supported, trained and equipped to serve effectively long term in potential foreign mission fields.

Hope in the Red-light District

Lang Lang was impressed with her friend, a dropout from her home village who was now living in the big city. She looked stylish and confident, her newest purchase was the most up-to-date cell phone money can buy. And she offered an opportunity: "It's an easy job and with a good salary! Come, and you can send lots of money home."

The offer was too much for Lang Lang to pass up. Only 15 years old, she, too, had dropped out of school and come to the city looking for work. Thus far, however, her job search had been futile. Desperate and hungry, she decided to go with her friend to work at the "massage parlor"—a brothel.

In a small room sat half a dozen girls, some lying on sofas and beds behind partitions, some busy putting on make-up or fake eyelashes. Their income is at least double what they could get as a salesperson. All they have to do is give up their bodies. But it comes at great cost.

It didn't take long for Lang Lang to realize her new job was not all her friend made it out to be, but she had financial obligations to her family. They thought she was working as a waitress. Finally, one day, she could stand it no longer.

She ran out of the parlor and into the street shouting, "I've had enough!" An angry customer and her boss followed, berating her and making threats.

Sherry happened to be walking by at the moment. Sherry and her co-workers run a Christian shelter and jewelry-making business that employs girls like Lang Lang, giving them a way out of prostitution. Sherry hugged Lang Lang and whispered, "If you don't want to work here, you have a choice. I can give you a job."

Two months later, Lang Lang sat at the table in the workroom, making jewelry. According to Sherry, she makes beautiful jewelry.

"How long will you stay here?" Sherry asked.

"I want to stay for quite a while … I want to reorganize my thoughts a little bit," Lang Lang replied. "I feel safe here."

Since arriving at the shelter, Lang Lang has received counseling and medical treatment to help recover from a sexually-transmitted disease. She's started studying the Bible daily. She even brought another friend who was looking for a way out of the brothels.

There have been setbacks as well. Twice, Lang Lang has run away. Thankfully, she's come back. She's now in charge of the jewelry business' storage room and is saving her money so she can go back to school one day.

The long-term goal of the shelter is to help girls recover mentally, physically and spiritually from the effects of prostitution. After two years in the shelter, the girls are encouraged to start a new life on their own, either through using their jewelry-making skills or through finding another legitimate job. They also go out with a new-found hope in their Lord and Savior, Jesus Christ.

恩典

Pray for Grace

Therefore, if anyone is in Christ, he is a new creation; the old has gone, the new has come!
2 Corinthians 5:17

» Ask for God's favor and blessing on this shelter, that it would be used by him to rescue many girls from a life of prostitution.

» Pray for the girls already engaged in or considering prostitution. Help them see the dangers and long-term scars and find new life and hope in Jesus Christ.

» Pray for those who benefit from prostitution (or exploitation of women) in China to repent and be changed by the gospel.

» Pray for more creative strategies like the jewelry business in reaching out to women and children at risk in China.

Life of a Child

"Xiao Chen, get up," says his mother. The clock reads 6:15 a.m. Xiao Chen is a 10-year-old living in one of China's mega cities. He slowly walks to the kitchen, where he eats a fried bread stick for breakfast.

With more promptings from his mother, he quickly puts on his school uniform, then returns to the table to study for his English test that day. A high score is expected. Xiao Chen's parents hope he will be able to attend a prestigious junior high and high school in the coming years—all in preparation for entrance into a prestigious college.

By 7:15, he's out the door, on his way to school. After school, he immediately heads to a one-hour piano lesson. He returns home shortly after five, when he has his only "free time" of the day. Most days, he uses the half hour to play a video game. After scarfing down dinner, it's back to the books. Two-to-three hours of homework is common for the fourth grader. He often breaks up the time with 30 minutes of piano practice. Exhausted, he falls asleep at 10 p.m. The day will begin early again tomorrow. The weekend offers some respite, except on Saturday morning when he goes to an English tutor.

Materially speaking, Xiao Chen lacks nothing. His father is a factory manager; his mother a professor. They are part of China's new and emerging upper middle class.

Like every one else his age, Xiao Chen is an only child. He lives with his parents and grandparents in a spacious apartment. Since birth, he has received everything he's ever wanted: toys, food, clothes. He lives at levels of comfort unseen by anyone but China's elite in previous generations.

But Xiao Chen's life of ease in one respect is balanced by high demands from his family. His parents have big plans for Xiao Chen. Maybe one day he could go to Beida or Tsinghua, the top two universities in China, then do graduate studies in the U.S. He could then return to China for a high-paying job, perhaps in business or engineering. It would be a good life—one that would bring the family much honor and esteem in the eyes of their friends and neighbors.

For now, that means Xiao Chen must endure an arduous regimen of study, school and extracurricular activities. His parents insist it's for his good. How else will he compete with other children doing the same thing?

China's generation of "Little Emperors," so named for the indulgent lifestyle lived by some of the children born under China's one-child policy, have a double-edged life. They are spoiled by parents and grandparents in some areas, but the trade off is a demand for academic excellence and a decrease in social life outside of school.

儿童

Pray for the Children

The thief comes only to steal and kill and destroy; I have come that they may have life, and have it to the full.
John 10:10

» Pray for Chinese children to have a healthy balance among school, extracurricular activities and home life.

» Pray for Chinese parents to have the wisdom and love needed to raise their children well.

» Lift up English programs and other outreaches by churches and foreign Christians that seek to communicate the gospel to Chinese youth. Ask that the hearts of these children would be fertile ground for the Good News.

New Place, New Hope

Graduating with a degree in engineering from Tsinghua University in Beijing, Zhang is one of the top minds in China. After graduation, he considered going immediately into the workforce, but he decided instead to apply to a graduate program at an American university. He arrived two years ago in the U.S. Nothing could have prepared him for the culture shock that followed. Zhang thought he spoke English pretty well—a high score on the TOEFL test seemed to confirm this thought—but being immersed in a completely English-speaking environment was different.

He struggled to find good, authentic Chinese food, like the food in his *laojia*, or hometown, in northern China. Zhang was also not accustomed to driving a car, but soon after arriving in the U.S., he learned this would be a necessity for his new life. One aspect of American culture he tried to understand was the devotion of his classmates to American-style football. On Saturdays in the fall, thousands of fans crammed into a stadium as big as the Bird's Nest in Beijing to cheer for the school's team. Zhang still didn't understand the rules, but he found the atmosphere exciting.

The hardest part, though, was the feeling of isolation. After his initial struggles at communicating with American classmates, Zhang eventually withdrew. He sometimes hung out with other Chinese students, especially at their Chinese New Year celebrations, but he longed for interaction with Americans. He wanted to know what their lives really looked like. How did they live? How did they celebrate holidays?

One day, an American man approached Zhang in the school's food court. He started asking Zhang where he was from and what he was studying. Zhang was taken aback by the man's friendliness, but also appreciative for some company. The two exchanged phone numbers. A week later, the man invited Zhang to his home for a Thanksgiving meal with his family.

Zhang leaped at the chance to celebrate an American holiday with an American family. Although he had been warned prior coming to China about American Christians, Zhang was intrigued when he heard his new friend speak about Jesus Christ. Zhang's life had been driven by a desire to succeed academically, professionally and financially. But this desire was never satisfied and ultimately felt empty and meaningless

Initially, it was hard to believe some of the man's claims—Zhang grew up an atheist, making the first verse in the Bible ("In the beginning, God created the heavens and the earth …") a leap of faith for him. But over time, his heart softened. He started going to a weekly Bible study for new believers and seekers.

The gospel truths struck a chord deep in Zhang's soul. Finally, one night, he could resist no longer. He cried out to God in faith and repented of his sin.

Zhang is still growing in his faith, but he is experiencing the deep and abiding joy of knowing his Savior. He now attends a Chinese church in the town where he is studying. In a couple of years, he hopes to return to China and be a godly influence and witness at a Chinese engineering company

By 2014, an estimated 550,000 Chinese students—high school, undergraduate and graduate—will be studying abroad.[1] One Chinese official has referred to these special students as "China's treasures." Christians worldwide have a golden opportunity to influence China with the gospel through these students.

---

1 chinadaily.com.cn, 4.25.11.

散居

Pray for the Scattered

That God was reconciling the world to himself in Christ, not counting men's sins against them. And he has committed to us the message of reconciliation.
2 Corinthians 5:19

» Pray for Chinese students to be receptive to the gospel while studying overseas.

» Ask God to call Christian families, churches and individuals in the West to seize the opportunity created by China's brightest minds studying in their communities and welcome them, sharing and demonstrating the love of Christ.

» Pray over the re-entry into China by Chinese students who become Christians while overseas. May they quickly find a good church and fellowship to encourage them in the faith.

Businessman, Missionary

John is a successful American businessman. He worked for 30 years in the shipping industry, advancing to the upper echelons in management of one of the top shipping companies in the world.

His success afforded him the opportunity to take early retirement. Instead of ending his working career, however, John re-invested his money and started his own business—in China.

For many years, John's heart for the Chinese people had grown. He now desired to leverage his years of business expertise and experience to be a light for the gospel. He wanted to demonstrate how to do his work with excellence, how to conduct business with integrity and how to treat his employees with dignity and respect. As he has lived out his faith in the workplace, God has opened many doors for John to share the good news and see personal transformation in employees who were sometimes accustomed to heavy-handed, corrupt bosses in their previous places of work.

John is part of a growing movement and strategy often referred to as missional business. Missional business involves reaching people for Christ through businesses centered in a missional purpose. Globalization has opened doors for Christian entrepreneurs and businessmen to start businesses—from micro-enterprises to more ambitious ventures—with the goal of not only producing a product, but also making a kingdom impact on employees and the surrounding community.

As a Communist country, China does not allow official "missionaries." There is no such thing as a "missionary visa," like those available in many other countries. This is why countries like China are often called creative access nations. A "missionary" in China has to have another, legitimate reason to be allowed in the country. This could mean studying Chinese (thus getting a student visa), teaching English (work visa) or doing business (work visa).

As a prime market for foreign investment, China is also ripe for the impact that missional business can bring. John regularly rubs shoulders with government officials and Chinese businessmen who crave the hope and salvation offered in the gospel. They have sought what the world has to offer and found it wanting. Without his business acumen, it is doubtful John would have such opportunities to impact segments of society that are harder to reach under the traditional missionary model.

It's not just nonbelievers that John is influencing, either. Through his life and work, John has inspired several Chinese Christian friends to view their own businesses and places of work as potential "mission fields."

商人

Pray for Businessmen

And whatever you do, whether in word or deed, do it all in the name of the Lord Jesus, giving thanks to God the Father through him.
Colossians 3:17

» Pray that more and more Christians in the West would take their professional and business skills to China in order to impact the nation with the gospel.

» Intercede for local and foreign Christians in China to have wisdom and direction in how to be a witness and run a viable business.

» Ask God to guide wise and effective partnerships between missional businesses and mission organizations ministering in China.

» Pray for Chinese people to be positively and eternally impacted by the lives of Christians in their workplace.

Next Steps

If God is leading you to involvement with his purposes in China, consider the following options:

Pray

"History belongs to the intercessors," someone once said. Use this booklet and other materials, such as requesting to receive a worker's prayer letter, to intercede for China on a regular basis.

Go

Short and long-term opportunities for going to China abound. Spend a summer in China teaching English, a year learning Chinese or a lifetime serving the Chinese people in various ways.

Welcome

Reach out to Chinese students at a nearby university or other Chinese you see in your neighborhood. Many Chinese temporarily living in the West long for interaction with local families and individuals.

Mobilize

Order one of these booklets for a friend or your church. Start a prayer group for China. Be an advocate for God's work in China.

Learn

Explore news sites and books related to China. Visit *www.omfbooks.com*. Inform yourself so you can be more effective in other areas of involvement.

Send

Partner with organizations or Christians working in China through the sharing of your time, money and other resources.

For more information on how you can be involved, go to ***www.omf.org.***

*Source list available upon request.